Chronicles of a Thirsty Traveler

An Allegory About the Source of the Water of Life

Julia L. Wise

TEACH Services, Inc.
PUBLISHING
www.TEACHServices.com • (800) 367-1844

Copyright © 2001 Julia L. Wise as "Searching for the Water of Life at the Big Spring"

Copyright © 2018 Julia L. Wise
Copyright © 2018 TEACH Services, Inc.
ISBN-13: 978-1-4796-0882-9 (Paperback)
ISBN-13: 978-1-4796-0883-6 (ePub)

Image Credits: Cover, proslgn; Intro., trans961; Chapter 1, Eva Alex; Chapter 2, olikli ; Chapter 2, schankz ; Chapter 3, rusak ; Chapter 4, rodakm ; Chapter 5, deberarr ; Chapter 5, rodimovpavel ; Back, Pongsakorn_jun – All from BigStockPhoto.com

TEACH Services, Inc.
PUBLISHING
www.TEACHServices.com ● (800) 367-1844

Table of Contents

1. The Energy Conserver.. 7

2. The Pretenders... 10

3. The Entrepreneur... 14

4. The Controller... 17

5. Water From The Rock.. 20

Introduction

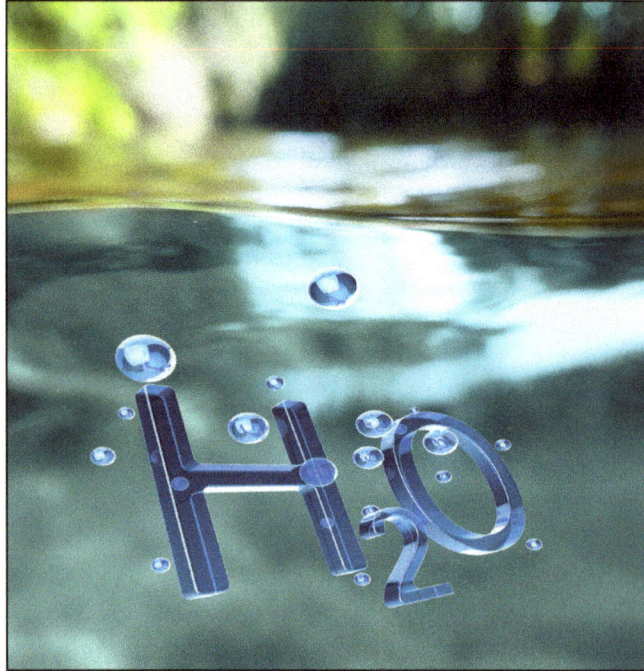

Thou visitest the earth, and waterest it: thou greatly enrichest it with the river of God, which is full of water: thou preparest them corn, when thou hast so provided for it. Thou waterest the ridges thereof abundantly: thou settlest the furrows thereof: thou makest it soft with showers: thou blessest the springing thereof. —Psalm 65:9, 10

Water—what an amazing blessing from God! And what a miracle each drop is! Think about the "recipe" for water—two molecules of a gas called hydrogen and one molecule of a gas called oxygen. Mix them together in the right way, and you have water. It's so essential to human life that we can't live without it for more than a few days. And what about every other living thing on the earth—plant or animal?

Related to the blessing of water is the blessing of thirst. The last time you were thirsty did you think of it as a blessing? Well, it was. Your brain was letting you know that it was past time to drink water. And, if you continued to ignore that warning, you got thirstier and thirstier until you did something about it.

We all know about physical thirst. But, have you ever thought about spiritual thirst? Is there something in the brain that "switches on" when it's time for a "spiritual drink of water?" Matthew 5:6 says, "Blessed are they which do hunger and thirst after righteousness: for they shall be filled." According to Jesus, it's good to be hungry and thirsty after righteousness. So, just as physical thirst is a gift from God, spiritual hunger and thirst must be also. Jeremiah 31:3 says, "The Lord hath appeared of old unto me, saying, Yea, I have loved thee with an everlasting love: therefore with loving kindness have I drawn thee." As we are drawn to Jesus by His unfailing love and follow wherever He leads, He will fill us with all we need, to grow into a vibrant, joyful Christian. One promise we can claim is found in Isaiah 49:10. "They shall not hunger nor thirst; neither shall the heat nor sun smite them: for he that hath mercy on them shall lead them, even by the springs of water shall he guide them."

Is there something in the brain that "switches on" when it's time for a "spiritual drink of water?"

CHAPTER 1

The Energy Conserver

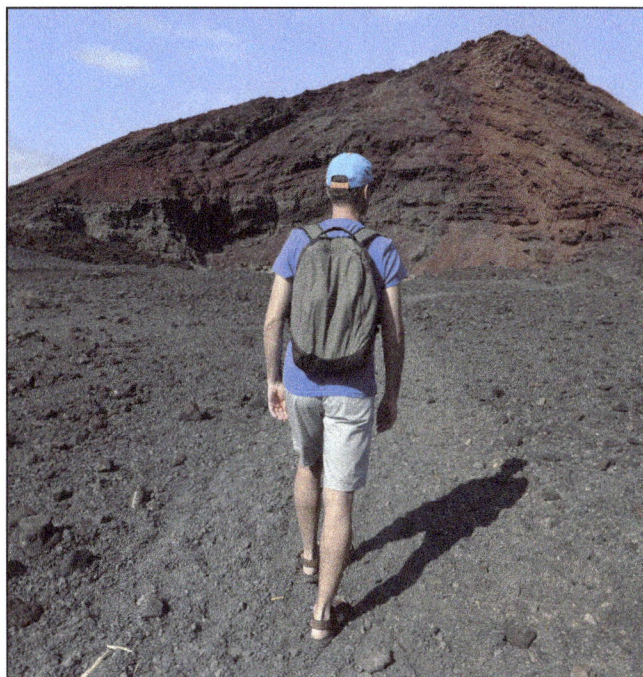

And the Spirit and the bride say, Come. And let him that heareth say, Come. And let him that is athirst come. And whosoever will, let him take the water of life freely.
—*Revelation 22:17*

Imagine with me a young person looking for a big spring. A friend has shared some of the water from the big spring with him, and he likes it so much that he can't wait to find the spring himself. His friend says that it isn't hard to find, but the person must follow the big spring guidebook to find the thirst-quenching water.

Picture the young person standing all alone in the desert one afternoon at the beginning of the road to the big spring, dressed in hiking clothes with a backpack full of travel food, two canteens of water, given by the friend, and camping gear. There is desolate terrain and a gravel road ahead. It looks fairly flat at first, climbs gently, then rises quickly, passing huge boulders, through foothills, and heading towards mountains in the distance. How long will the journey take? It doesn't matter. The young person has come prepared for the journey, bringing the guidebook that he has promised to follow to the letter!

> *For my people have committed two evils; they have forsaken me the fountain of living waters, and hewed them out cisterns, broken cisterns, that can hold no water.*
> —Jeremiah 2:13

Could it be that you have found water already?

Now, imagine that *you* are that young person. It is you who is standing at the beginning of the trail in the middle of a desert. You are holding canteens of water in your backpack as you are ready to start your journey—a slight breeze blowing on this very warm day. You put on your hat, adjust your pack, grab your walking stick, and start walking, reading your guidebook as you move along. The book tells just where to find the big spring. All you need to do is to stay on the strait and narrow road, ignoring the side roads.

Following the road for two hours or so, you see a sign scribbled in crayon on a weathered piece of wood that you can barely read. It says: "WATER" and it has an arrow pointing to the right. The weathering tells you that the sign has been there awhile—the hot sun melting the wax of the scribbled lettering. Your heart skips a beat. Could it be that you have found water already? Ignoring the advice of your guidebook, you decide to investigate. Your steps quicken as you leave the main gravel road and turn down the faint path that takes you through the dry brush and down rocky terrain.

After walking half a mile, you notice an outcropping of rocks, underneath which is a shallow cave. As you approach, you see a hammock strung between two wooden supports. There is a man in the hammock, dozing in the late afternoon sun with an ancient cowboy hat covering his face. His tan shirt is stained and frayed. His jeans are also in tatters, and he hasn't even bothered to take off his boots.

You don't want to bother him, but it is almost suppertime, so you call out, "Hello!" The man doesn't move. You come a little closer. "Hello," you say again. "I'm looking for water. Can you help me?" Slowly the man lifts the hat from off his face and sits up to look at you. He has a week's worth of stubble, and his greasy black hair sticks out in all directions.

"Water? Did you say you needed water?" he says. "Well, yes, I have water. See that cement water tank over yonder? Go help yourself. Then come back so we can sit and visit. Not many people stop by my place."

About thirty feet away you spot a cistern. But, as you get closer, you hear what sounds like the croaking of a frog. What? Frogs in the desert? How is that possible? Reaching the water tank, you look around for a cup. You spot a plastic bottle on a branch of a nearby scrubby bush. The warped wooden cover of the cistern is slightly askew as you pull it aside to scoop out some water. Just then, the croaking stops and you hear a plop and a swampy smell fills the air. Inside there is green scum floating on top of the water down at the bottom of the cistern. There are also chunks of cement breaking away from the sides of the wall. You dip the bottle into the green water and lift it up for inspection. The smell is overwhelming. Who would ever drink water like this? It is nothing like the fresh, cool water given you by your friend. Where is that water?

You put the cover back on the cistern and walk back to the man in the hammock. Noticing a convenient rock, you sit down.

"Did you find the water?" he asks.

"Yes, I did," you reply, purposely not saying, "Thank you." Then you ask sheepishly, "Could I ask where you got your water?"

"Well, about two months ago I borrowed a donkey and cart and took a large barrel to the big spring where I filled the barrel with water. When I got home, I emptied the barrel into my water tank. It took ten nights to fill it up. My, that water always tastes good! But, I suppose the water in my cistern is getting a might old. Soon as I run out, I'll go get me some more."

"Where is the big spring?" you say. "I would like to go there myself."

"Just go back to the strait and narrow road, stay on it, and you'll find it. It's a bit of a hike though."

Curious as to why he was here, you ask, "You mentioned earlier that this was your 'place.' Do you live here?"

"Why, yes, I do."

"Why don't you move closer to the big spring so you won't have so far to go to get water? Aren't you lonely living way out here in the middle of nowhere?"

"Live closer to the big spring, you say? Well, I used to live closer a while back, but I decided to move. The people there were way too happy, and there was always something going on. So I moved out here, cleaned up a spot in the cave, and made a fire pit and a place to store water. When I need food, I hitch a ride into town. Otherwise, I keep busy sweeping out my cave and trimming the sagebrush around the entryway. When all my work is done, I can just relax in the sunshine."

You look around and see that the cave is deeper than you at first had thought. A door of rough boards stands ajar at an opening towards the rear of the front part of the cave. You are not impressed with his "house" and neither are you impressed with his landscaping talents.

He continues, "No, I don't want to live too close to the big spring. They might put me to work. Living out here I can share what I have with anyone who wanders off the main path, without interrupting everything else I have to do. Say, it's about suppertime. Would you like to stay and eat?"

He starts to dish out some wilted salad greens from a rusted tin and saws off a couple of slices from a stale loaf of bread.

"No, thank you," you say, "I must be on my way." Then you tip your hat and retrace your steps to the main road.

Apparently, a person shouldn't count on yesterday's water. You've got to take the time to get it fresh every day.

A glance at your watch tells you that it's ten after five. There's still time to walk awhile before it gets dark. A bit hungry despite seeing the man's unappetizing food, you pull out an apple and some trail mix. Munching on these, you continue your journey. And, oh, the water in your canteen tastes so good! But you have to be careful not to waste it. It has got to last you until you get to the big spring.

CHAPTER 2

The Pretenders

Jesus answered, Verily, verily, I say unto thee, Except a man be born of water and of the Spirit, he cannot enter into the kingdom of God. —John 3:5

On you walk for another two hours. The winding road starts a gentle climb. A sign announces: "Welcome. We have water. Come enjoy it with us." The sign is painted on red wooden boards with purple lettering and a yellow floral border. *A bit garish*, you muse to yourself. You know that you should stay on the strait and narrow, but the sun is going down, and you need a place to stay for the night.

Curious, you take the road to the left, passing another large sign, which says, "Turn here and enjoy some water with us." The road, oddly, is wider than the strait and narrow, and its hard-packed gravel is easy to walk on. Several yards along, another sign announces, "Water, a quarter mile farther." *Somebody sure aims to please*, you say to yourself, as you continue eagerly down the road.

The road curves right and then left. As you top a hill, you see what looks like a small oasis in the desert. Could it be? Do they have the water that you are looking for? The oasis has green grass, palm trees, and even a few orange and lemon trees. Also, a large, beautiful, blue pool of water. There is a row of five rustic cabins and three tents. What a feast for the eyes after walking hours in the desert! As you approach the oasis, you hear laughter and the soft strumming of a guitar.

A man sees you and quickly walks over to greet you. "Welcome, come join us," he says warmly, shaking your hand firmly.

"Don't mind if I do," you say, as you survey the scene.

The sun has just set, and a cool breeze is blowing. About twenty people are sitting around a table beneath a grass-roofed pavilion. Lanterns are lit one by one, giving the place a feeling of the tropics.

She quickly mixes the "improved" sparkling water in a beautifully carved wooden cup, and hands it to you.

After you find a seat, a young lady walks over and says, "We're glad that you are with us," and hands you a brightly-colored menu with a confusing list of water choices. It takes you a few moments to figure it out.

Step one is "Choose your flavor." *Hmm, there's artificial lemon, artificial lime, artificial strawberry, and seven other artificial flavors*, you think as you read.

Step two is "Choose your herb, vitamin, and mineral mix." The list of ailments that it claims to treat is impressive. There are mixtures to help increase or decrease appetite, mixtures to increase energy or calm your nerves, and mixtures to help you fall asleep or wake up.

Step three is "Choose your level on the 'sparkle' spectrum—'just a touch,' 'regular,' or 'super-charged.'"

"Do you have any plain water?" you ask.

"Well, no," she answers. "All we serve is 'improved' water."

"OK," you reply, as you scan the list of choices again. "I'll take the artificial lime, rejuvenating water with the regular 'sparkle.'"

She quickly mixes the "improved" sparkling water in a beautifully carved wooden cup, and hands it to you.

"Thank you," you say, putting the cup to your mouth and drinking deeply of the cool liquid. Ugh! The water is so carbonated that it burns all the way down your throat. The lady sitting next to you stops her lively chatter and says, "Oh, you must be very thirsty! Would you like some more?"

"No, thank you," you say in a choked voice. "I have had enough for now. But I would like to know why it is that you don't serve plain water here."

"Well, that's easy to explain," she says. "It's because of the quality of our water. We have a water treatment plant to filter and purify the water, but, as much as we have tried, we can't quite get rid of the bitter taste. That's why we offer multiple flavors and levels of carbonation. And, our water doesn't just cover the off-taste—we have a long list of healthy supplements to choose from. So, we are serving a product that is actually *better* than pure water. Besides, who wants plain water anymore? *Plain* is rather boring, don't you think?"

She doesn't stop long enough to let your respond.

"We've started this retreat to encourage people to drink water. Along with the choices of water, we have invested in guest tents, cabins for employees, an upgraded access road, and extensive advertising. People can stop by, make their selection of water, and sit and visit awhile, or they can order their preference of water, in bulk, for delivery. If they have traveled far, they can stay overnight. It's much more *convenient* than going all the way to the big spring."

"Thanks for explaining. I would like to visit more, but I really need a place to rest for the night. Do you have anything available?"

"Yes, we do," she says. "Tent number three is empty tonight. You can borrow this lantern for the night, to see your way over to the tent. I think you will find it quite comfortable. Just make yourself at home."

"Thanks so much and good night," you say as you take the lantern and head toward the tent.

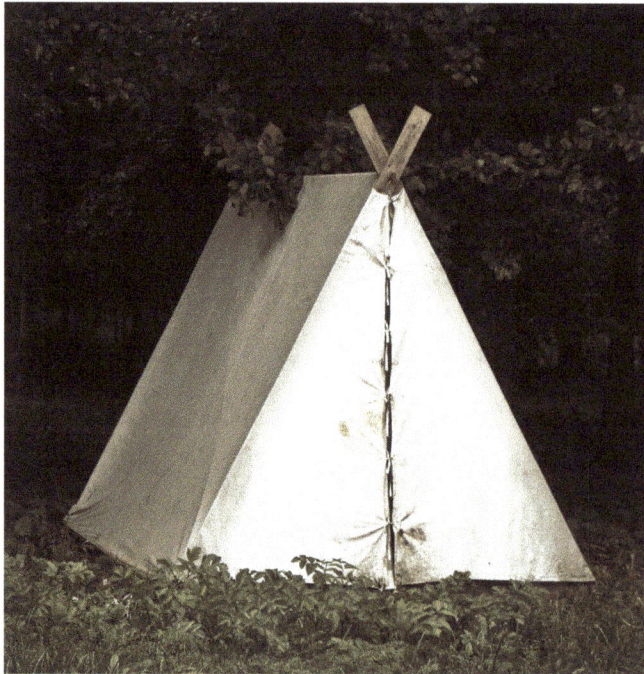

Walking the short distance to the tent, you lift the canvas flap and look inside. There are two cots, one on each side, with a small table in the middle. You step up on the wood plank floor and set the lantern on the table. Weary from the day's travel, you shut off the lantern, spread your sleeping bag on one of the cots, and snuggle up inside, drifting off to sleep to the distant sound of voices and music.

The next morning, as the sun is just beginning to peak over the horizon, you look around. *Where am I? Oh, now I remember...* The only sounds you hear are the gentle rustle of the wind through the leaves and the occasional twitter of a bird. Maybe, if you are quiet, you can get on your way before anyone else wakes up, and maybe they won't mind if you pick an orange to add to your breakfast. They did say for you to make yourself at home.

Rolling out of your sleeping bag, you pack your things and then quickly pen a thank you note to leave on the table. Hoisting your pack on your back, you drop your pen, and it rolls on the floor and out the front flap of the tent. As you are retrieving your pen, your hand brushes against the grass. It isn't real; it's artificial turf. *Well, that certainly cuts down on labor in mowing*, you think to yourself.

Then you go for that orange. The one you grab doesn't feel right. Well, no wonder—it isn't real. It's made of wax, the orange tree itself is plastic, and the palm trees are artificial too. So, you have walked on artificial grass, picked artificial fruit, and—worst of all—drunk artificially "improved" water! What is this place? There is no time to figure it out, but now you realize that appearances can certainly be deceiving and that you won't be satisfied until you get the real thing. Water from a different source—even when "improved"—is no substitute.

Traveling back up the smooth gravel road, you snack on a bit of trail food, and return to the strait and narrow. It feels good to be on the road to the big spring. Maybe you will have some of its good water by tonight. That encouraging thought inspires you to go on.

CHAPTER 3

The Entrepreneur

For by grace are ye saved through faith; and that not of yourselves: it is the gift of God: Not of works, lest any man should boast. —Ephesians 2:8, 9

Two-and-a-half hours down the road, it is now 9:30, and the sun is now heating things up. You put on your hat to keep the sun off your face.

How much farther is it to the big spring? Sure hope it's soon.

Just then you hear a rumbling sound. It is very faint at first and then, as you pass a huge boulder, it gets much louder. It sounds like heavy equipment, like bulldozers and cranes. You don't have long to wonder. Ten minutes later you see a yellow sign beside the road that says, "Caution, men working," with a sandy, deeply rutted road to the right. A little way off the road stands another sign with bold blue lettering on a white background that says, "Water Works Project." Curious, you decide to take a look.

Down the deeply rutted road you go. Not far along, you see another sign that says "Office" next to an arrow pointing left. So you head that way. You are almost to the sidewalk that leads to the door of the impressive big office building when a man walks out the door. He is big and muscular and walks with a gait that says that he means business.

"Well, howdy," he says with a smile. "What brings you to these here parts?"

"I am looking for water and I saw your sign, so I stopped to check this place out."

"If it's water you're looking for, you've come to the right place. Let me get us a couple of hardhats, and I'll show you the operation."

He dashes inside the building and is back in a moment with the hats. We walk alongside the building. As you pass the back corner, you see some raised beds in the backyard. Several trays of assorted vegetable plants stand wilting under the sun.

"Are you growing a garden?" you ask.

"That's the plan," the man replies.

You continue along the road together a short distance and, as you reach the top of a hill, you gasp! For a half a mile or more, all you can see is pile after pile of sand and gravel. Beside each pile is a great gaping hole. Several cranes are digging more holes and making more piles of sand and gravel. Several bulldozers are making roads requiring the cranes to make still more holes and piles.

"Quite an operation, don't you think?" he says with a grin. "We work very hard here. It takes a lot of work to make big piles of sand and gravel beside the holes."

"But what about the water?" you ask. "The sign said, 'Water Works Project.'"

"Yes, that's just what we're doing. We're working very hard to get water. Sometimes we even get wet sand. But I expect sooner or later we'll get water."

"Have you ever spent time reading the directions about how to find the best water?" you ask.

"You mean the directions in the guidebook to the big spring?" he replies.

"Yes," you say.

"Oh that," he says. "I have one back in my office. I've read some of it, but I'm too busy digging to read it now. I do remember it saying that the big spring is at the end of the strait and narrow road."

You stare at him for a moment. Is what he is saying possible? He knows how to get to the spring, yet he digs here.

You summon all your courage and finally ask him the obvious, "If the water is at the end of the road, why are you looking for water here?"

You almost feel sorry for asking as his shoulders sag and he sheepishly says, "You ask a right hard question. I've always thought that, if I worked hard enough, I would find my *own* source of water. That way I won't have to

"If it's water you're looking for, you've come to the right place."

be dependent on someone else for water. Also, I will get the credit for finding it. So far, I have to admit, I haven't been successful."

Then he turns and starts back for the office, with you silently in pursuit.

As you almost reach the office, he says, "Would you like to come in and visit?"

"No, thank you," you reply. "I must be on way to the big spring. Maybe you'll come some time too?"

He nods his head and smiles. As you turn and head back to the strait and narrow road, you see him wave and then turn back to his work.

Apparently, if a person ignores the guidebook, it's easy to spend a lot of time and energy looking for water in the wrong place.

You breathe a sigh of relief—you're back on track again. The hour visiting with the workman was a waste, but if you hurry maybe you can get a few miles behind you before lunch—and maybe even find the big spring by then! You didn't press the workman for water. Even if he did have some, he certainly wouldn't have had enough to share with you.

CHAPTER 4

The Controller

But woe unto you, scribes and Pharisees, hypocrites! For ye shut up the kingdom of heaven against men: for ye neither go in yourselves, neither suffer ye them that are entering to go in.—Matthew 23:13

The morning wears on. As the sun grows hotter, you get thirstier and thirstier. You drink sparingly from your canteen to make the water last. The sun reaches its peak and starts toward the west. The road is starting to narrow, and you notice it getting continually steeper. You have just about decided to stop and eat your lunch when you see another sign. This one is very small and it has very small lettering. It would have been easy to have missed it. Printed neatly on a shiny piece of metal, it reads, "Water, get it here from the big spring." The "big spring"! You can't wait to taste it as you imagine that first big swallow of water.

You follow the steep trail to the left. It is so steep in parts that it has steps carved into the rock. Up and around corners you go until, at last, you reach the top of the hill and see a little stone house. You knock on the door, and a neatly dressed man of slight build opens the door.

"What are you doing here?" he inquires.

"I saw the sign for water from the big spring and thought maybe someone here could help me. Can you?"

"Just a minute, come on in."

He motions for you to sit in a chair as he goes over to the cupboard, looking for something to put water in.

As the sun grows hotter, you get thirstier and thirstier.

It takes your eyes awhile to adjust to the darkness inside his house. You notice that, though all his belongings are in perfect order, they are covered in a thick layer of dust. You also notice the centerpiece on the kitchen table. It is a bowl of fruit, which must have been fresh at one time, but it certainly is not any more. The fruit is all shriveled—the plums have become prunes, the grapes have become raisins, and these also are covered in a blanket of dust. The drapes are drawn; the room smells musty. It has been a long time since fresh air and sunshine have entered this room.

The man walks over to you carrying two small tin cups. "I was just about ready to go get some water myself. Let's go."

You walk a short distance from his house.

"Where's the big spring?" you ask excitedly, almost tasting the refreshing water.

"The big spring isn't here. I just bring water in from it."

"Oh," you say. *Oh no*, you think, remembering your recent "cistern" experience. Then he reaches down and starts turning something. You bend down and see what you hadn't noticed before. There is a pipe on the ground with a spigot attached to it. He turns it all the way on, holds his small tin cup to catch the water, and a trickle of water comes out.

"Oh dear," he sighs. "I guess I have to check the pipes again for leaks."

"What pipes are those?" you ask.

"Those pipes," he says, as he points up towards the next hill. You look up and see a great system of pipes, partially covered with dirt and rocks, going up the next hill and then the one after that.

"Where do they go?"

"To the big spring, of course!" He looks at you with disdain. "And I've installed a pump to control the water pressure. I thought that all I had to do was keep the pump working, and I would have all the water I wanted. But the pipes seem to spring a leak so often that I end up spending a lot of time fixing them."

"Is the big spring far from here?"

"Well, no, it isn't."

"So, why don't you go directly to the source of the life-giving water?"

"Why would I go there when I can pipe it over here? And here I can control how much water I get and who I give it to by the twist of a knob. When I don't want any more I just turn it off. That way I don't waste a drop. Over at the big spring, there is so much water that folks keep spilling it all the time. And anyone who is thirsty can come to get some."

Hmm. Anyone can come.... Now, that's a thought!

He finishes filling your small cup and hands it to you. You drink it quickly and then look up. At first it tastes good, but after the last swallow, you notice a strong metallic aftertaste—quite unpleasant. But you are still thirsty, so you ask, "Could I have some more, please?"

"Well, OK," the man says begrudgingly. "I'll give you one more cup, but that's all for now."

You linger as long as you can over the second small cup, but it disappears before you know it. The man has already started back toward his house. Without looking back, he says, "I'll walk you partway back so's I can get my tools and see what's wrong with the plumbing. I've got to take care of this myself."

You have discovered that, even if the water you have drunk came from the true source of life-giving water, if it passes through a man-made delivery system, the amount you get is not enough and the piping adds its own tainted flavor to the water.

You hurry to catch up with him. At his house, you bid him good-bye and walk down the steep, winding path towards the strait and narrow road.

CHAPTER 5

Water From The Rock

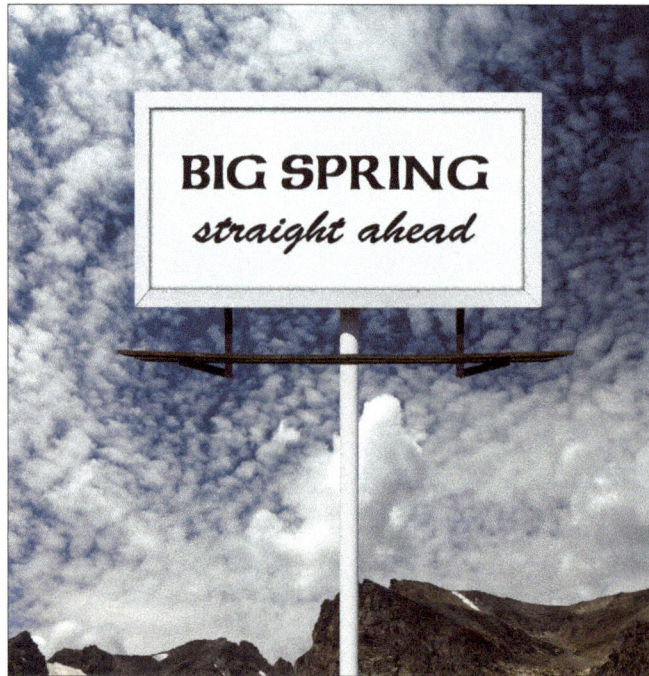

Enter ye in at the strait gate: for wide is the gate, and broad is the way, that leadeth to destruction, and many there be which go in thereat: Because strait is the gate, and narrow is the way, which leadeth unto life, and few there be that find it. —Matthew 7:13, 14

Once you get back to the main road, you find a rock to sit on, and you eat an apple and some trail mix. You also take a swallow of your dwindling supply of water. Then you pull out your guidebook and scold yourself for not having read it more often. You review the part that says, "Stay on the strait and narrow until you come to the big spring." After your late lunch, you feel refreshed and get going again on the strait and narrow.

About a half hour later, you find that you can't walk as fast as you had been because the road isn't as smooth as it was before, and sometimes you have to walk around big boulders in the way. You must be getting close by now. And then you see it—a large white sign that is simply lettered, "BIG SPRING straight ahead." Your step regains its bounce as you think about the spring's cool, clear water. Although the road is steep and full of barriers, you almost don't notice. The air seems fresher and there is a fragrance in the air with the aroma of flowers. Now the road flattens out as you walk around one last big boulder, and there it is—an oasis in the high desert with vibrant green grass, blossoming orange trees, and date palms loaded with fruit. Then you see it—the spring—the big flowing spring, cascading out of a mighty rock in the mountain and pooling in a large hollow just below. A breeze drifts toward you, carrying with it the cooling mist rising from the pool. Looking up, you see a beautiful rainbow as the afternoon sun shines through the rising mist. Drawing closer to the spring, you notice several benches. Sitting on the one nearest you, you disentangle yourself from your pack, close your eyes, and breathe in the invigorating air. It feels so good to be here! Then you open your eyes and see crowds of people gathered about, talking, smiling, and drinking the sparkling water from the ever-flowing spring. Little children are running and playing and filling the air with the sweet sound of their laughter. There is a long table laden with fresh, delectable fruit.

Your step regains its bounce as you think about the spring's cool, clear water.

A Man with kind eyes and a beard hands you a glass filled to the top with fresh spring water and says, "Here, drink your fill; there is always more if you want more. We have a never-ending supply of water here, to receive for the asking." You take the first glass, and then you get more and more until your thirst is gone. Finally, you have found the true water of life. You need look no further. Your journey has come to its end. Whenever you want fresh, pure water, there is no other place to get it. Jesus told the woman at the well, "Whosoever drinketh of the water that I shall give him shall never thirst; but the water that I shall give him shall be in him a well of water springing up into everlasting life" (John 4:14).

* * * *

In reality, you and I don't have to literally travel daily through the desert, to receive the water of life from Jesus. He is as close to us as a prayer. The Psalmist says, "The Lord is nigh unto all them that call upon him, to all that call upon him in truth" (Psalm 145:18). So, we can daily drink the water of life, as we prayerfully talk to Jesus, and meditate on His Word. As we grow with Jesus, He will make changes in our lives, from the inside, that we will praise Him for. Paul describes it this way in Colossians 1:27, "...the riches of the glory of the mystery among the Gentiles; which is Christ in you, the hope of glory."

* * * *

So, now that you know where the water is, what's stopping you from taking a cupful from the Man with the beard and the kind eyes?